quail studio

Published by Quail Publishing Limited
Office 10, The Incuba, 1 Brewers Hill Road, Dunstable,
Bedfordshire, LU6 1AA, United Kingdom

ISBN: 978-0-9935908-4-9

We have made every effort to ensure the accuracy and
completeness of these instructions. We cannot, however, be
responsible for human error, typographical mistakes, or varia-
tions in individual work.

Art Editor: Georgina Brant
Graphic Design: Quail Studio
Photography: Jesse Wild
Technical Lead: Emma Brant
Yarn Support: Rowan Yarns
Designer: Dee Hardwicke

British Library Cataloguing in Publication Data
A catalogue record for this book is available from the
British Library

Printed in the United Kingdom

colourwork
knits

12 HAND KNIT DESIGNS
INSPIRED BY NATURE

Dee
Hardwicke

quail studio

contents

introduction

I'm endlessly inspired by the beauty of the natural world and by the colours, textures and patterns of the changing seasons. I find inspiration everywhere, from childhood memories of sunny Sundays spent sitting outside painting flowers, to romantic autumn walks through city parks, and happy afternoons watching beautifully colourful butterflies flit from plant to plant in my garden.

Plants and flowers become intertwined with some of our most precious memories, and as an artist and knitter I love the process of transforming the transient, everchanging beauty of nature and those special moments into knitted designs to treasure for years to come. This passion has led me to hold regular workshops where I guide participants through every step of creating an intarsia quilt featuring motifs of their favourite plants and flowers, and is the subject of my book 'A Story in Yarn: How to Design and Knit an Intarsia Heirloom Quilt'.

In the same way that a quilt can tell a story and be something to treasure, so can a garment. In 'Colourwork Knits', I take you through the techniques and inspirations behind my first knitwear collection. Each garment is based on the shapes I love to wear, from a perfectly fitted cardigan in rich colours that evoke thoughts of a sunny evening walk, to gorgeous, roomy sweaters to wrap yourself up in on colder days.

My butterfly pom pom shawl is the perfect piece to add a warm splash of colour to an outfit, and and you'll always have happy memories of chilly days spent wearing the textured and stylish hydrangea knitted coat, hat and scarf.

I hope you enjoy knitting these designs for yourself or for your friends and family as much as I've loved creating them. They're very much intended to be worn and to add joy and colour to everyday life, and I hope they'll also become interwoven with your happiest, most treasured memories.

Dee Hardwicke

circle flowers sweater
page. 32

boyfriend scarf
page. 38

boyfriend
sweater

page. 44

*butterfly
skirt*

page. 52

dee motif
cardigan
page. 58

*heart leaf
boxy jumper*

page. 66

hydrangea
flower coat
page. 72

*oak leaf
yoke top*

page. 84

*pom pom
shawl*

page. 90

spring blossom cardigan
page. 94

the patterns

circle flowers sweater

Designed in Rowan Valley Tweed
Hardraw (108)
Littondale (102)
Gordale (105)

circle flowers sweater

YARN

Rowan Valley Tweed

A Hardraw 108

5	5	6	6 x 50gm

B Littondale 102

2	2	2	3 x 50gm

C Gordale 105

1	1	2	2 x 50gm

NEEDLES

1 pair 2¾mm (no 12) (US 2) needles
1 pair 3¼mm (no 10) (US 3) needles
1 2¾mm (no 12) (US 2) circular needle 40cm / 16in long
1 3¼mm (no 10) (US 3) circular needle, one 40cm / 16in long and one 60cm / 24in long

TENSION

24 sts and 36 rows to 10cm / 4in measured over st st, using 3¼mm (US 3) needles.

EXTRAS

Stitch holders

BACK

Using 2¾mm (US 2) needles and yarn B, cast on 118 (130: 142: 154) sts.

Row 1 (RS): K2, *P2, K2, rep from * to end.

Row 2: *P2, K2, rep from * to last 2 sts, P2.

These 2 rows form rib.

Cont in rib until back meas 4cm / 1½in, ending with **WS** facing for next row.

Next row (WS): P1, M1, purl to last st, M1, P1.

120 [132: 144: 156] sts.

Break off yarn B.

Change to 3¼mm (US 3) needles.

Place chart

Using the **intarsia** and **Fair Isle** techniques as described on the information page, now place patt from chart A, (please note: side shapings are **NOT** shown on the chart), which is worked entirely in st st beg with a K row, as folls:

Next row (RS): Using yarn C, K0 (6: 0: 6), (work next 24 sts as row 1 of chart A) 5 (5: 6: 6) times, using yarn C, K0 (6: 0: 6).

Next row: Using yarn C, P0 (6: 0: 6), (work next 24 sts as row 2 of chart A) 5 (5: 6: 6) times, using yarn C, P0 (6: 0: 6).
These 2 rows set the sts – chart A, with st st in yarn C at each side.
Keeping sts correct as now set, dec 1 st at each end on foll 7th row. 118 [130: 142: 154] sts.
Work 17 rows straight, ending with RS facing for next row.
All 26 rows of chart A are now completed.
Break off yarns B and C.
Using yarn A **only,** cont in st st and dec 1 st at each end of 5th and every foll 22nd row to 110 (122: 134: 146) sts.
Cont straight until back meas 30 (31: 32: 33)cm/
11¾ (12¼, 12½, 13)in ending with RS facing for next row.

Shape armholes
Cast off 4 (6: 6: 8) sts at beg of next 2 rows.
102 [110: 122: 130] sts.
Dec 1 st at each end of next row, and on foll 2 (3: 4: 4) alt rows. 96 [102: 112: 120] sts.
Work 1 row, ending with RS facing for next row.
Leave these sts on a holder.

FRONT

Work as given for back until 6 (4: 4: 4) rows less have been worked than on back to beg of armhole shaping, ending with RS facing for next row.

Shape front neck
Next row (RS): K35 (41: 47: 53), and turn, leaving rem sts on a holder.
Work each side of neck separately.
Next row: Cast off 5 (6: 6: 7) sts, purl to end.
30 [35: 41: 46] sts.
Next row: Knit to last 2 sts, K2tog.
29 [34: 40: 45] sts.
Next row: Cast off 4 (5: 5: 7) sts, purl to end.
25 [29: 35: 38] sts.
For 1st size only
Next row: Knit to last 2 sts, K2tog. 24 sts.
Next row: Cast off 3 sts, purl to end. 21 sts.
For all sizes
Shape armhole
Cast off 4 (6: 6: 8) sts at beg and dec 1 st at end of next

row. 16 [22: 28: 29] sts.
Next row: Cast off 3 (4: 5: 6) sts, purl to end.
13 [18: 23: 23] sts.
Next row: K2tog, knit to last 2 sts, K2tog.
11 [16: 21: 21] sts.
Next row: Cast off 3 sts, purl to end.
8 [13: 18: 18] sts.
Rep last 2 rows, 1 (2: 3: 3) times more. 3 sts.
Next row: K2tog, K1. 2 sts.
Next row: P2tog. Fasten off.
With RS facing, slip centre 40 sts onto another holder, rejoin yarn A, and cast off 5 (6: 6: 7) sts, knit to end.
30 [35: 41: 46] sts.
Complete to match first side, reversing shapings.

SLEEVES

Using 2¾mm (US 2) needles and yarn C, cast on 58 (58: 62: 62) sts.
Work in rib as given for back until sleeve meas 8cm / 3¼in, ending with **WS** facing for next row.
Next row (WS): P1, M1, purl to last st, M1, P1.
60 [60: 64: 64] sts.
Break off yarn C.

Change to 3¼mm (US 3) needles.
Place chart
Using the **intarsia** and **Fair Isle** techniques as described on the information page, now place patt from chart B, (please note: side shapings are **NOT** shown on the chart), which is worked entirely in st st beg with a K row, as folls:
Next row (RS): Using yarn B, K0 (0: 2: 2), (work next 20 sts as row 1 of chart B) 3 times, using yarn B, K0 (0: 2: 2).
Next row: Using yarn B, P0 (0: 2: 2), (work next 20 sts as row 2 of chart B) 3 times, using yarn B, P0 (0: 2: 2).
These 2 rows set the sts – chart B, with st st in yarn B at each side.
Keeping sts correct as now set, work 4 rows, ending with RS facing for next row.
Next row(RS): K1, M1, knit to last st, M1, K1.
62 [62: 66: 66] sts.
Last row sets increases.
Working increases as set by last row, inc 1 st at each end on 2 foll 6th rows. 66 [66: 70: 70] sts.
Work 1 row, ending with RS facing for next row.
All 20 rows of chart B are now completed.
Break off yarns B and C.

Using yarn A **only,** cont in st st and inc I st at each end
of 7th (5th: 5th: 5th) and every foll 8th (6th: 6th: 6th) row
to 88 (74: 76: 94) sts, then on foll – (8th: 8th: 8th) row until
there are – (92: 96: 100) sts.

Cont straight until sleeve meas 43 (43: 44: 44)cm /
17 (17, 17¼, 17¼)in, ending with RS facing for next row.

Shape top

Cast off 4 (6: 6: 8) sts at beg of next 2 rows.
80 [80: 84: 84] sts.

Dec I st at end of next row, and on foll 2 (3: 4: 4) alt rows.
74 [72: 74: 74] sts.

Work I row, ending with RS facing for next row.
Leave these sts on a holder.

MAKING UP

Press as described on the information page.
Join all raglan seams using mattress stitch.

Yoke and neckband

With RS facing, using longer 3¼mm (US 3) circular needle
and yarn B, slip first 48 (51: 56: 60) sts on back holder onto
another holder, then Knit across rem 48 (51: 56: 60) sts, K
across 74 (72: 74: 74) sts on left sleeve holder dec – (-: -: I)
st at beg and end, pick up and knit 18 (18: 20: 19) sts down
left side of front neck, K across 40 sts from front neck
holder dec – (I: -: I) st at beg and end, pick up and knit
18 (18: 20: 19) sts up right side of front neck, K across
74 (72: 74: 74) sts on right sleeve, dec – (-: -: I) st at beg
and end, then K across rem 48 (51: 56: 60) sts of back.
320 [320: 340: 340] sts.

Using the **intarsia** and **Fair Isle** techniques as described
on the information page, repeating the 20-st patt rep
16 (16: 17: 17) times around each round, work I to 32
rows in patt from chart C **once**, which is worked entirely
in st st (K every round).
Break off B and C.

Using A **only,** work as folls, changing to shorter 3¼mm
(US 3) circular needle when required:

Round I: *K8, SI I, K I, psso, rep from * to end.
288 [288: 306: 306] sts.

Work 5 rounds.

Round 7: *K2tog, K7, rep from * to end.
256 [256: 272: 272] sts.

Work 5 rounds.

Round 13: *K6, SI I, K I, psso, rep from * to end.
224 [224: 238: 238] sts.

Work 3 (3: 3: 5) rounds.

Round 17(17,17,19): *K2tog, K5, rep from * to end.
192 [192: 204: 204] sts.

Work 3 rounds.

Round 21(21,21,23): *K4, SI I, K I, psso, rep from * to
end. 160 [160: 170: 170] sts.

Work 3 rounds.

Round 25(25,25,27): *K2tog, K3, rep from * to end.
128 [128: 136: 136] sts.

Break off yarn A, join in yarn C.

Change to 2¾mm (US 2) circular needle.

Next round: Knit.

Next round: *K2, P2, rep from * to end.

Rep last round 11 times more.

Cast off in rib.

Join side and sleeve seams using mattress stitch.

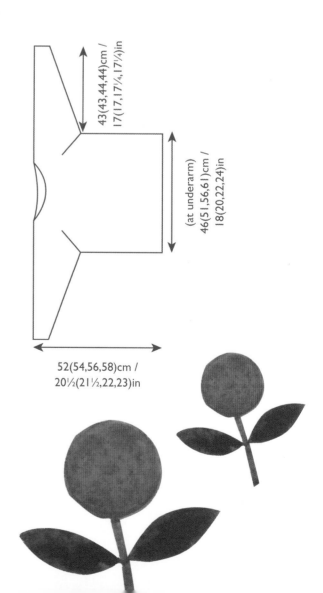

43(43,44,44)cm /
17(17,17¼,17¼)in

(at underarm)
46(51,56,61)cm /
18(20,22,24)in

52(54,56,58)cm /
20½(21½,22,23)in

Chart A (Body Chart)

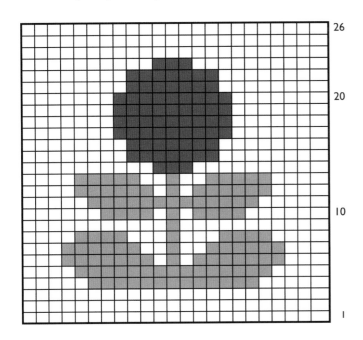

26
20
10
1

Body Key

☐ Gordale
■ Hardraw
■ Littondale

Chart C (Yoke Chart)

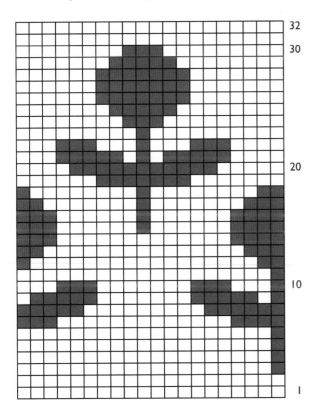

32
30
20
10
1

Chart B (Sleeve Chart)

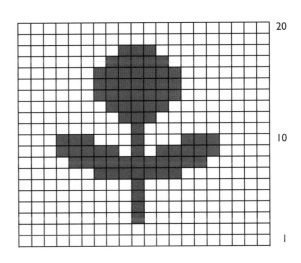

20
10
1

Yoke & Sleeve Key

☐ Littondale
■ Hardraw
■ Gordale

boyfriend scarf

Designed in Rowan Alpaca Soft DK
Rainy Day (210)
Marine Blue (212)
Toffee (203)

boyfriend scarf

SIZE

One size

31cm /12¼ in x 206cm / 81in (excluding pom poms)

YARN

Rowan Alpaca Soft DK

A Rainy Day 210
7 x 50gm

B Marine Blue 212
2 x 50gm

C Toffee 203
1 x 50gm

NEEDLES

1 pair 3¾mm (no 9) (US 5) needles
1 pair 4mm (no 8) (US 6) needles

TENSION

22 sts and 30 rows to 10cm / 4in measured over st st, using 4mm (US 6) needles.

EXTRAS

Pom pom maker.

Using 3¾mm (US 5) needles and yarn A, cast on 71 sts.
Next row (RS): *K1, P1, rep from * to last st, K1.
Last row sets moss st.

Work in moss st as set for a further 17 rows.

Change to 4mm (US 6) needles.
Beg and ending rows as indicated, using the intarsia technique as described on the information page, cont in patt from chart, which is worked entirely in st st beg with a K row, as folls:
Row 1: (RS) (K1, P1) twice, K1, work next 61 sts as row 1 of chart, K1, (P1, K1) twice.
Row 2: (K1, P1) twice, K1, work next 61 sts as row 2 of chart, K1, (P1, K1) twice.
Working rows as set, cont straight until 194 rows of chart have been worked 3 times.

Change to 3¾mm (US 5) needles.
Next row: (RS) *K1, P1, rep from * to last st, K1.
Last row sets moss st.
Work in moss st as set for a further 17 rows

MAKING UP
Press as described on the information page.
Using yarn C, make 10 pom poms approx 5cm / 2in in diameter.
Attach 5 pom poms evenly along the cast-on and cast-off edges.

Chart (Continued)

Key

☐ Rainy Day

▨ Toffee

■ Marine Blue

boyfriend sweater

Designed in Rowan Alpaca Soft DK
Marine Blue (212)
Rainy Day (210)
Toffee (203)

boyfriend
sweater

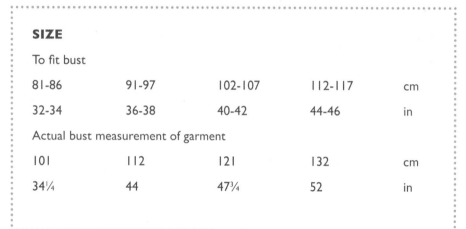

SIZE

To fit bust

| 81-86 | 91-97 | 102-107 | 112-117 | cm |
| 32-34 | 36-38 | 40-42 | 44-46 | in |

Actual bust measurement of garment

| 101 | 112 | 121 | 132 | cm |
| 34¼ | 44 | 47¾ | 52 | in |

YARN

Rowan Alpaca Soft DK

A Marine Blue 212

| 8 | 9 | 10 | 10 | x 50gm |

B Rainy Day 210

| 3 | 3 | 3 | 3 | x 50gm |

C Toffee 203

| 2 | 2 | 2 | 2 | x 50gm |

NEEDLES

1 pair 3¼mm (no 10) (US 3) needles
1 pair 4mm (no 8) (US 6) needles

TENSION

22 sts and 30 rows to 10cm / 4in measured over st st, using 4mm (US 6) needles.

EXTRAS

Stitch Holder

BACK

Using 3¼mm (US 3) needles and yarn C, cast on 122 (134: 146: 158) sts.
Row 1: (RS) K2, *P2, K2, rep from * to end.
Row 2: *P2, K2, rep from * to last 2 sts, P2.
These 2 rows form rib.
Work in rib until back meas 11cm / 4¼in, ending with **WS** facing for next row.
Next row: (WS) Purl to end, inc (inc: dec: dec) 1 st at end of row. 123 [135: 145: 157] sts.

Change to 4mm (US 6) needles.
Beg and ending rows as indicated, using the **intarsia** technique as described on the information page, cont in patt from chart, which is worked entirely in st st beg with a K row, as folls:
Dec 1 st at each end of 9th and every foll 12th row to 111 (123: 133: 145) sts.
(Please note: side shaping is **NOT** shown on the chart).
Cont straight until chart row 146 (152: 158: 164) has been completed, ending with RS facing for next row.
Back should meas approx. 59.5 (61.5: 63.5: 65.5)cm / 23½ (24¼: 25: 25¾)in.)

Shape back neck

Next row: (RS) K37 (43: 47: 53), and turn, leaving rem sts on a holder.

Work each side of neck separately.

Dec 1 st at neck edge on next 3 rows. 34 [40: 44: 50] sts.

Shape shoulder

Cast off 16 (19: 21: 24) sts at beg of next row, **and at same time** dec 1 st at neck edge. 17 [20: 22: 25] sts.

Work 1 row.

Cast off rem 17 (20: 22: 25) sts.

With RS facing, slip centre 37 (37: 39: 39) sts onto a holder, rejoin appropriate yarn and patt to end.

Complete to match first side, reversing shapings.

FRONT

Work as given for back until chart row 120 (126: 128: 134) has been completed, ending with RS facing for next row.

Shape front neck

Next row: (RS) K41 (47: 52: 58) sts and turn, leaving rem sts on a holder.

Work each side of neck separately.

Dec 1 st at neck edge on next 4 rows, then on foll 4 (4: 5: 5) foll alt rows. 33 [39: 43: 49] sts.

Work 17 (17: 19: 19) rows straight.

Shape shoulder

Cast off 16 (19: 21: 24) sts at beg of next row. 17 [20: 22: 25] sts.

Work 1 row.

Cast off rem 17 (20: 22: 25) sts.

With RS facing, slip centre 29 sts onto a holder, rejoin appropriate yarn and patt to end.

Complete to match first side, reversing shapings.

SLEEVES

Using 3¼mm (US 3) needles and yarn C, cast on 50 (50: 54: 54) sts.

Work in rib as given for back for 11cm / 4¼in, ending with **WS** facing for next row.

Next row: (WS) Purl to last 2 sts, P2tog.

49 [49: 53: 53] sts.

Change to 4mm (US 6) needles.

Beg and ending rows as indicated, using the **intarsia** technique as described on the information page, cont in patt from sleeve chart working left sleeve from left sleeve chart and right sleeve from right sleeve chart, which is

worked entirely in st st beg with a K row, as folls:

Work 6 rows, ending with RS facing for next row.

(Please note: side shaping is **NOT** shown on the chart).

Next row: (RS) K1, M1, knit to last st, M1, K1.

51 [51: 55: 55] sts.

Last row sets increases.

Working increases as set by last row, inc 1 st at each end on every foll 8th (6th: 6th: 6th) row to 63 (53: 61: 77) sts, then on every foll 10th (8th: 8th: 8th) row until there are 77 (81: 87: 91) sts.

Work 7 rows straight, ending after chart row 132 (132: 136: 136] and with RS facing for next row.

Shape top

Cast off 7 (8: 8: 9) sts at beg of next 4 rows.

49 [49: 55: 55] sts.

Cast off 8 (8: 9: 9) sts at beg of next 4 rows.

Cast off rem 17 (17: 19: 19) sts.

MAKING UP

Press as described on the information page.

Join right shoulder seam using mattress stitch.

Neckband

With RS facing, using 3¼mm needles and yarn C, pick up and knit 22 (22: 25: 25) sts down left side of front neck, knit across 29 sts on front holder, pick up and knit 22 (22: 25: 25) sts up right side of front neck, pick up and knit 4 sts down right side of back neck, knit across 37 (37: 39: 39) sts on back holder, then pick up and knit 4 sts up left side of back neck.

118 [118: 126: 126] sts.

Next row: (WS) Purl.

Work in rib as given for back for 9cm / 3½in, ending with RS facing for next row.

Cast off in rib.

Join left shoulder and neckband seams using mattress stitch.

Mark points along side seam edges 21 (22: 23: 24)cm / 8¼ (8¾: 9: 9½)in, either side of shoulder seam (to denote base of armhole openings).

Sew in sleeves.

Join side and sleeve seams.

61.5(63.5,65.5,67.5)cm /
24¼(25,25¾,26½)in

55(55,56,56)cm /
21¾(21¾,22,22)in

(at underarm)
50.5(56,60.5,65.5)cm /
20(22,23¾,25¾)in

Key

☐ Rainy Day

▨ Toffee

■ Marine Blue

Chart - All sizes

Left Sleeve

136
130
120
110
100
90
80
70
60
50
40
30
20
10
1

L & XL   S & M   S & M   L & XL

butterfly skirt

Designed in Rowan Valley Tweed
Janet's Foss (110)
Bedale (106)
Gordale (105)
Wolds Poppy (107)

butterfly skirt

SIZE

To fit hip

XS/S	M/L	XL/XXL	

Actual hip measurement of skirt

68½	75	85	cm
27	29½	33½	in

YARN

Rowan Valley Tweed

A Janet's Foss 110

5	5	6	x 50gm

B Bedale 106

1	1	1	x 50gm

C Gordale 105

1	1	1	x 50gm

D Wolds Poppy 107

1	1	1	x 50gm

NEEDLES

1 pair 3¼mm (no 10) (US 3) needles
1 pair 3.25mm (no 10) (US 3) needles

TENSION

24 sts and 36 rows to 10 cm / 4in measured over st st, using 3¼mm (US 3) needles.

SKIRT

(Work 2 pieces)

Using 3¼mm (US 3) needles and yarn A, cast on 146 (166: 190) sts.

Row 1 (RS): K2, *P2, K2, rep from * to end.

Row 2: *P2, K2, rep from * to last st, P2.

These 2 rows form rib.

Work in rib until work meas 10 cm / 4in, inc(dec: dec) 1 st in centre of last row and ending with RS facing for next row. 147 [165: 189] sts.

Beg and ending rows as indicated, using the **intarsia** technique as described on the information page, cont in patt from chart,

(please note side shapings are **NOT** shown on chart), which is worked entirely in st st beg with a K row as folls:

Dec 1 st at each end of 5th and then every foll 6th row to 109 (127: 151) sts, then on every foll 8th row to 101 (119: 143) sts.

Work 6 rows straight, ending with **WS** facing for next row. (Should meas approx. 52cm / 20½in).

Next row: (WS) Using yarn D, P4 (2: 10), P2tog, (P3 [2: 1], P2tog) 18 (28: 40) times, P5 (3: 11). 82 [90: 102] sts.
Break off yarn D.

Using yarn A **only,** and beg with row 1 of 2x2 rib, work for 8cm / 3¼in, ending with RS facing for next row.
Cast off in rib.

MAKING UP

Press as described on the information page.
Join side seams using mattress stitch.

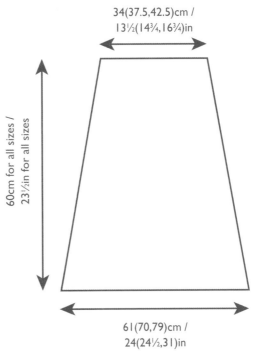

34(37.5,42.5)cm /
13½(14¾,16¾)in

60cm for all sizes /
23½in for all sizes

61(70,79)cm /
24(24½,31)in

Chart

Key

☐ Janet's Foss

▨ Bedale

▨ Gordale

▨ Wolds Poppy

XS/S   M/L   XL/XXL

dee motif cardigan

Designed in Rowan Valley Tweed

Wolds Poppy (107)

Malham (101)

Janet's Foss (110)

dee motif cardigan

SIZE

To fit bust

81-86	91-97	102-107	112-117	cm
32-34	36-38	40-42	44-46	in

Actual bust measurement of garment

85	96.5	108	117	cm
33½	38	42½	46	in

YARN

Rowan Valley Tweed

A Wolds Poppy 107

4	4	5	5	x 50gm

B Malham 101

1	1	1	1	x 50gm

C Janet's Foss 110

1	1	1	1	x 50gm

NEEDLES

1 pair 2¾mm (no 12) (US 2) needles
1 pair 3¼mm (no 10) (US 3) needles

TENSION

24 sts and 36 rows to 10cm / 4in measured over st st, using 3¼mm (US 3) needles.

EXTRAS

11 buttons
Stitch holders

BACK

Using 2¾mm (US 2) needles and yarn B, cast on 87 (101: 115: 125) sts.

Join in yarn A.

Row 1 (RS): K1, *P1, K1, rep from * to end.

Row 2: *P1, K1, rep from * to last st, P1.

These 2 rows form rib.

Joining in and breaking off colours as required, cont in rib in stripes as folls:

Rows 3 to 12: Using yarn A.

Row 13: Using yarn B.

Rows 14 to 26: Using yarn A.

Rows 27 to 40: As rows 13 to 26.

Row 41: Using yarn B.

Row 42 to 53: Using yarn A.

Row 54: Using yarn A, purl to last st, M1, P1.

88 [102: 116: 126] sts.

Change to 3¼mm (US 3) needles.

Beg and ending rows as indicated, using the **intarsia** technique as described on the information page, work rows

1 to 14 in patt from body chart **once**, which is worked entirely in st st beg with a K row.

Break off yarns B and C.

Using yarn A **only,** cont in st st as folls:

Work 2 rows, ending with RS facing for next row.

Next row (RS): K1, M1, knit to last st, M1, K1. 90 [104: 118: 128] sts.

Last row sets increases.

Working increases as set by last row, inc 1 st at each end on every foll 6th row to 102 (116: 130: 140) sts.

Cont straight until back meas 34 (32.5: 34.5: 33) cm / 13½ (12¾: 13½: 13) in, ending with RS facing for next row.

Shape armholes

Cast off 4 (4: 5: 5) sts at beg of next 2 rows. 94 [108: 120: 130] sts.

Dec 1 st at each end of next 3 (5: 7: 9) rows, then on foll 2 (4: 5: 5) alt rows. 84 [90: 96: 102] sts.

Cont straight until armhole meas 18 (19.5: 21: 22.5) cm / 7¾(7½: 8¼: 8¾) in, ending with RS facing for next row.

Shape shoulders and back neck

Next row (RS): Cast off 8 (10: 11: 12) sts, K until there are 20 (21: 22: 24) sts on right needle and turn, leaving rem sts on a holder.

Work each side of neck separately.

Dec 1 st at neck edge on next 2 rows **and at same time** cast off 9 (10: 10: 11) sts at beg of 2nd row. 9 [9: 10: 11] sts.

Work 1 row.

Cast off rem 9 (9: 10: 11) sts.

With RS facing, rejoin yarn to rem sts, cast off centre 28 (28: 30: 30) sts, K to end. 28 [31: 33: 36} sts.

Complete to match first side, reversing shapings.

LEFT FRONT

Using 2¾mm (US 2) needles and yarn B, cast on 50 (56: 64: 68) sts.

Join in yarn A.

Row 1 (RS): K1, *P1, K1, rep from * to last st, K1.

Row 2: K1, *P1, K1, rep from * to last st, P1.

These 2 rows form rib.

Joining in and breaking off colours as required, cont in rib in stripes as folls:

Rows 3 to 12: Using yarn A.

Row 13: Using yarn B.

Rows 14 to 26: Using yarn A.

Rows 27 to 40: As rows 13 to 26.

Row 41: Using yarn B.

Rows 42 to 53: Using yarn A.

Row 54: Using yarn A, K1, (P1, K1) 3 times, purl to last – (1: -: 1) st, (M1, P1) – (1: -: 1) times. 50 [57: 64: 69] sts.

Change to 3¼mm (US 3) needles.

Beg and ending rows as indicated, using the **intarsia** technique as described on the information page, work rows 1 to 14 in patt from fronts chart **once**, which is worked entirely in st st beg with a K row.

Row 1 (RS): Work 43 (50: 57: 62) sts as row 1 of front chart, (P1, K1) 3 times, K1.

Row 2: K1, (P1, K1) 3 times, work next 43 (50: 57: 62) sts as row 2 of front chart.

These 2 rows set the sts – front opening edge 7 sts still in rib, with all other sts now in st st working from body chart. Keeping sts correct as now set, work rows 3 to 14 of body chart.

Break off yarns B and C.

Using yarn A **only,** cont in st st as folls:

Work 2 rows, ending with RS facing for next row.

Next row (RS): K1, M1, knit to last 7 sts, (P1, K1) 3 times, K1. 51 [58: 65: 70] sts.

Last row sets increases.

Working increases as set by last row, inc 1 st at beg of every foll 6th row to 57 (64: 71: 76) sts.

Cont straight until left front meas 34 (32.5: 34.5: 33) cm / 13½ (12¾: 13½: 13) in, ending with RS facing for next row.

Shape armhole

Cast off 4 (4: 5: 5) sts at beg of next row. 53 [60: 66: 71] sts.

Work 1 row.

Dec 1 st at armhole edge of next 3 (5: 7: 9) rows, then on foll 2 (4: 5: 5) alt rows. 48 [51: 54: 57] sts.

Cont straight until 44 (44: 48: 48) rows less have been worked than on back to beg of shoulder shaping, ending with RS facing for next row.

Shape front neck

Next row (RS): K41 (44: 47: 50), and turn, leaving rem 7 sts on a holder (for yoke).

Dec 1 st at neck edge on next 4 rows, dec 1 st at neck edge on foll 7 alt rows, then 4 (4: 5: 5) foll 4th rows. 26 [29: 31: 34] sts.

Work 9 rows straight, ending with RS facing for next row.

Shape shoulder

Cast off 8 (10: 11: 12) sts at beg of next row, then 9 (10: 10: 11) sts at beg of foll alt row.

Work 1 row.

Cast off rem 9 (9: 10: 11) sts.

Mark position for 11 buttons along left front opening edge – first button to come in row 5, last 3 buttons will be positioned in the yoke and neckband – first to come in row 5, second in row 22, then in row 38 and rem 7 buttons evenly spaced between these.

RIGHT FRONT

Using 2¾mm (US 2) needles and yarn B, cast on 50 (56: 64: 68) sts.

Join in yarn A.

Row 1 (RS): K2, *P1, K1, rep from * to end.

Row 2: *P1, K1, rep from * to end.

These 2 rows form rib.

Joining in and breaking off colours as required, cont in rib in stripes as folls:

Rows 3 and 4: Using yarn A.

Row 5 (buttonhole row) (RS): K2, P1, yon, work 2tog, rib to end.

Working a further 7 buttonholes in this way to correspond with positions marked for buttons on left front and noting that no further reference will be made to buttonholes, cont as folls:

Rows 6 to 12: Using yarn A.

Row 13: Using yarn B.

Rows 14 to 26: Using yarn A.

Rows 27 to 40: As rows 13 to 26.

Row 41: Using yarn B.

Rows 40 to 53: Using yarn A.

Row 54: Using yarn A, (P1, M1) -(1: -: 1) times, purl to last 7 sts, (K1, P1) 3 times, K1. 50 [57: 64: 69] sts.

Change to 3¼mm (US 3) needles.

Beg and ending rows as indicated, using the **intarsia**

technique as described on the information page, work rows 1 to 14 in patt from fronts chart **once**, which is worked entirely in st st beg with a K row.

Row 1 (RS): K1, (K1, P1) 3 times, work next 43 (50: 57: 62) sts as row 1 of front chart.

Row 2: Work 43 (50: 57: 62) sts as row 2 of front chart, (K1, P1) 3 times, K1.

These 2 rows set the sts – front opening edge 7 sts still in rib with all other sts now in st st working from front chart. Keeping sts correct as now set, work rows 3 to 14 of front chart.

Break off yarns B and C.

Using yarn A **only,** cont in st st as folls:

Work 2 rows, ending with RS facing for next row.

Next row (RS): K1, (P1, K1) 3 times, knit to last st, M1, K1. 51 [58: 65: 70] sts.

Last row sets increases.

Working increases as set by last row, inc 1 st at end of every foll 6th row to 57 (64: 71: 76) sts.

Complete to match left front, reversing shapings and working first row of neck shaping as folls:

Next row (RS): Patt 7 sts and slip these sts onto a holder, patt to end. 41 [44: 47: 50] sts.

SLEEVES

Using 2¾mm (US 2) needles and yarn A, cast on 47 (49: 53: 53) sts.

Work in rib as given for back working stripes as folls:

Rows 1 to 10: Using yarn A.

Row 11: Using yarn B.

Rows 12 to 21: Using yarn A.

Row 22 (WS): Using yarn A, purl to end, inc 2 sts evenly across row. 49 [51: 55: 55] sts.

Change to 3¼mm (US 3) needles.

Place chart

Beg and ending rows as indicated, using the **intarsia** technique as described on the information page, now place sleeve chart, which is worked entirely in st st beg with a K row.

Next row (RS): Using yarn B, K2 (3: 5: 5), (work 15-st patt rep as row 1 of sleeve chart) 3 times, using yarn B, K2 [3: 5: 5].

Next row: Using yarn B, P2 (3: 5: 5), (work 15-st patt rep as row 2 of sleeve chart) 3 times, using yarn B, P2 (3: 5: 5).

These 2 rows set the sts – 45 sts in patt from chart, with edge sts still in st st using yarn B.

Work as set for a further 12 rows, ending with RS facing for next row.

Break off yarns B and C.

Using yarn A **only,** cont in st st as folls:

Next row (RS): K1, M1, knit to last st, M1, K1.

51 [53: 57: 57] sts.

Last row sets increases.

Working increases as set by last row, inc 1 st at each end on every foll 6th (6th: 6th: 4th) row to 65 (73: 81: 67) sts, then on every foll 8th (8th: 8th: 6th) row until there are 75 (79: 85: 89) sts.

Cont straight until sleeve meas 36 (37: 38: 38) cm / 14 (14½: 15: 15) in, ending with RS facing for next row.

Shape top

Cast off 4 (4: 5: 5) sts at beg of next 2 rows.

67 [71: 75: 79] sts.

Dec 1 st at each end of next 3 rows, then on 7 (8: 10: 12) foll alt rows, then on 3 (4: 4: 4) foll 4th rows. 41 sts.

Work 1 row, ending with RS facing for next row.

Dec 1 st at each end of next and 2 foll alt rows, then on foll 4 rows. 27 sts.

Work 1 row, ending with RS facing for next row.

Cast off 3 sts at beg of next 2 rows, then 4 sts at beg of next 2 rows.

Cast off rem 13 sts.

MAKING UP

Press as described on the information page.

Join shoulder seams using mattress stitch.

Yoke and neckband

With RS facing, using 3¼mm (US 3) needles and yarn B, patt across 7 sts from right front holder, pick up and knit 34 (34: 35: 35) sts up neck edge of right front, 37 (37: 39: 39) sts from back neck, pick up and knit 34 (34: 35: 35) sts down neck edge of left front, then patt across 7 sts on left front holder. 119 [119: 123: 123] sts.

Place chart

Beg and ending rows as indicated, using the **intarsia** technique as described on the information page, now place yoke chart, which is worked entirely in st st

beg with a **P** row.

Row 1 (WS): K1, (P1, K1) 3 times, P0 (0, 2, 2) sts, work next 105 sts as row 1 of yoke chart, P0 (0, 2, 2) sts, (K1, P1) 3 times, K1.

Row 2: K1, (K1, P1) 3 times, K0 (0, 2, 2) sts, work 105 sts as row 2 of yoke chart, K0 (0, 2, 2) sts, (P1, K1) 3 times, K1. These 2 rows set the sts – front opening edge 7 sts still in rib, with all other sts now in st st working from yoke chart. Work a further 3 rows from yoke chart.

Row 6 (buttonhole row) (RS): K2, P1, yon, work 2tog, work to end.

Work 6 rows more from chart B.

Break off yarn C, join in yarn B.

Row 13 (WS): Using yarn B, K1, (P1, K1) 3 times, P to last 7 sts, (K1, P1) 3 times, K1.

Change to 2¾mm (US 2) needles.

Row 14: Using yarn A, K1, (K1, P1) 3 times, K to last 7 sts, (P1, K1) 3 times, K1.

Row 15: Using yarn A, (K1, P1) to last st, K1.

Row 16: Using yarn A, K1, (K1, P1) to last 2 sts, K2. Repeating rows 15 and 16, work a further 11 rows in A, 1 row in B, and 14 rows in A **and at the same time** work buttonholes as before in row 22 and 38, ending with RS facing for next row. Cast off in rib.

Using mattress stitch, sew in sleeves.

Join side and sleeve seams.

Sew on buttons.

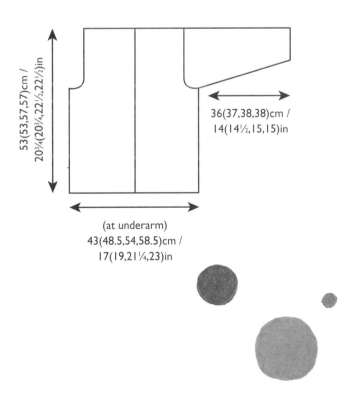

53(53,57,57)cm / 20¾(20¾,22½,22½)in

36(37,38,38)cm / 14(14½,15,15)in

(at underarm) 43(48.5,54,58.5)cm / 17(19,21¼,23)in

Back and Fronts

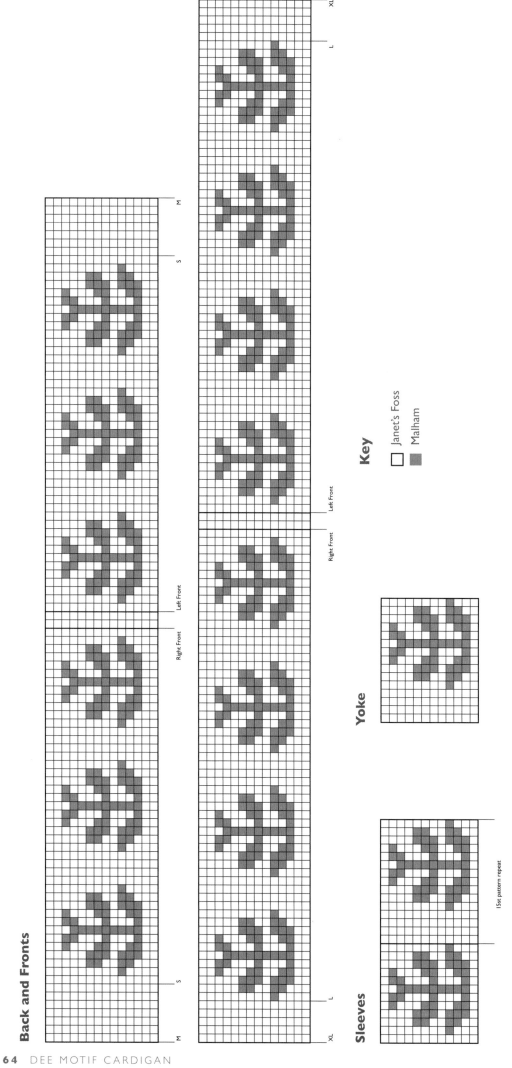

Left Front

Right Front

Right Front

Left Front

M   S   S   M

XL   L   L   XL

XL   L   L   XL

Key

☐ Janet's Foss
▨ Malham

Yoke

Sleeves

15st pattern repeat

heart leaf boxy jumper

Designed in Rowan Felted Tweed
Clay (177)
Seasalter (178)
Avocado (161)
Watery (152)
Frozen (185)
Rage (150)
Mineral (181)

heart leaf boxy jumper

SIZE

To fit bust

81-86	91-97	102-107	112-117	cm
39½	43½	47½	51½	in

Actual bust measurement of garment

100	110	120	130	cm
39¼	43¼	47¼	51¼	in

YARN

Rowan Felted Tweed

A Clay 177

4	4	5	5	x 50gm

B Seasalter 178

1	1	1	1	x 50gm

C Avocado 161

1	1	1	1	x 50gm

D Watery 152

1	1	1	1	x 50gm

E Frozen 185

1	1	1	1	x 50gm

F Rage 150

1	1	1	1	x 50gm

G Mineral 181

1	1	1	1	x 50gm

NEEDLES

1 pair 3¾mm (no 9) (US 5) needles.
1 pair 4mm (no 8) (US 6) needles.

TENSION

22 sts and 30 rows to 10cm / 4in measured over st st, using 4mm (US 6) needles.

EXTRAS

Stitch holders.

BACK
Using 3¾mm (US 5) needles and yarn A, cast on 111 (121: 133: 143) sts.
Row 1 (RS): K1, *P1, K1, rep from * to end.
Row 2: *P1, K1, rep from * to last st, P1.
These 2 rows form rib.
Joining in and breaking off colours as required, cont in rib in stripes as folls:
Rows 3 and 4: Using yarn B.
Rows 5 and 6: Using yarn C.
Rows 7 and 8: Using yarn D.

Rows 9 and 10: Using yarn E.

Rows 11 and 12: Using yarn F.

Row 13: Using yarn G.

Row 14: Using yarn G, purl to end, P2tog.
110 [120: 132: 142] sts.

Break off yarns B, C, D, E, F and G.

Change to 4mm (US 6) needles.

Using yarn A, work as folls:

Row 1 (RS): Knit.

Row 2: K1, purl to last st, K1.

Last 2 rows set st st with edge sts.

Cont as set above for a further 4 rows, ending with RS facing for next row.

Place motif chart

Beg and ending rows as indicated, using the **intarsia** technique as described on the information page, now place chart, which is worked entirely in st st beg with a K row.

Next row (RS): Using yarn D, K10 (15: 21: 26), work next 90 sts as row 1 of motif chart, using yarn B, K10 (15: 21: 26).

Next row. Using yarn B, K1, P9 (14: 20: 25), work next 90 sts as row 2 of motif chart, using yarn D, P9 (14: 20: 25), K1.

These 2 rows set the sts – centre 90 sts in patt from chart for motif with edge sts still using yarns D and E.

Working rem 43 rows of chart.

Completing the back using yarn A, cont as folls:

Row 1 (RS): Knit.

Row 2: K1, purl to last st, K1.

Last 2 rows set st st with edge sts. Cont straight as set above until back meas 26.5 (27: 27.5: 28)cm / 10½ (10¾, 10¾, 11)in, ending with RS facing for next row.

Shape armholes

Dec 1 st at each end of next 5 (5: 6: 6) rows.
100 [110: 120: 130] sts.

Cont straight until armhole meas 20 (21.5: 23: 24.5)cm / 7¾ (8½, 9, 9¾)in, ending with RS facing for next row.

Shape shoulders and back neck

Next row (RS): Cast off 10 (12: 13: 15) sts, K until there are 22 (25: 28: 31) sts on right needle and turn, leaving rem sts on a holder.

Work each side of neck separately.

Dec 1 st at neck edge on next 2 rows **and at same time** cast off 10 (12: 13: 15) sts at beg of 2nd row.
10 [11: 13: 14] sts.

Work 1 row.

Cast off rem 10 (11: 13: 14) sts.

With RS facing, slip centre 36 (36: 38: 38) sts onto a holder, rejoin yarn A to rem sts, K to end.

Complete to match first side, reversing shapings.

FRONT

Work as given for back until 20 (20: 22: 22) rows less have been worked than on back to beg of shoulder shaping, ending with RS facing for next row.

Shape front neck

Next row (RS): K39 (44: 49: 54) and turn, leaving rem sts on a holder.

Work each side of neck separately.

Dec 1 st at neck edge on next 4 rows, dec 1 st at neck edge on foll 5 (5: 6: 6) alt rows. 30 [35: 39: 44] sts.

Work 5 rows straight.

Shape shoulder

Cast off 10 (12: 13: 15) sts at beg of next row, and foll alt row. 20 [23: 26: 29] sts.

Work 1 row.

Cast off rem 10 (11: 13: 14) sts.

With RS facing, slip centre 22 sts onto a holder, rejoin yarn A to rem sts, K to end.

Complete to match first side, reversing shapings.

SLEEVES

Using 3¾mm (US 5) needles and yarn A, cast on 53 (55: 57: 57) sts.

Work in rib and stripe sequence as given for back.

Break off yarns B, C, D, E, F and G.

Change to 4mm (US 6) needles.

Using yarn A, work as folls:

Row 1 (RS): Knit.

Row 2: K1, purl to last st, K1.

Last 2 rows set st st with edge sts.

Cont as set above for a further 2 rows, ending with RS facing for next row.

Next row (RS): K1, M1, knit to last st, M1, K1.
55 [57: 59: 59] sts.

Last row sets increases.

Working increases as set by last row,

inc 1 st at each end of every foll 10th (8th: 6th: 6th) row to 67 (71: 63: 87) sts, then on every foll 12th (10th: 8th: 8th) row until there are 73 (79: 85: 91) sts.

Cont straight until sleeve meas 43 (43: 44: 44)cm / 17 (17, 17¼, 17¼)in, ending with RS facing for next row.

Shape top

Dec 1 st at each end of next 5 (5: 6: 6) rows.

63 [69: 73: 79] sts.

Work 1 (1: 0: 0) row, ending with RS facing for next row.

Cast off 3 (4: 4: 4) sts at beg of next 2 (8: 14: 8) rows, then 4 (5: -: 5) sts at beg of next 10 (4: -: 6) rows.

Cast off rem 17 sts.

MAKING UP

Press as described on the information page.

Join right shoulder seam using mattress stitch.

Neckband

With RS facing and using 3¾mm (US 5) needles and yarn A, pick up and knit 21 (21: 23: 23) sts down left side of front neck, knit across 22 sts on front holder, pick up and knit 22 (22: 24: 24) sts up right side of front neck, pick up and knit 3 sts down right side of back neck, knit across 36 (36: 38: 38) sts on back holder, then pick up and knit 3 sts up left side of back neck.

107 [107: 113: 113] sts.

Beg with row 2 of rib as given for back, work 1 row in rib.

Joining in and breaking off colours as required,

cont in rib in stripes as folls:

Rows 3 and 4: Using yarn B.

Rows 5 and 6: Using yarn C.

Rows 7 and 8: Using yarn D.

Rows 9 and 10: Using yarn E.

Rows 11 and 12: Using yarn F.

Rows 13 and 14: Using yarn G.

Rows 15 and 16: Using yarn A.

Rows 17 to 29: As rows 3 to 15.

Cast off in rib (on a **WS** row).

Join left shoulder and neckband seams.

Sew in sleeves.

Join side and sleeve seams.

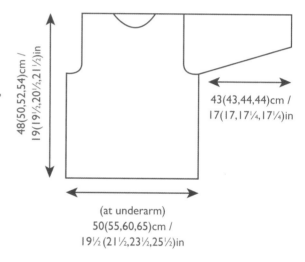

43(43,44,44)cm / 17(17,17¼,17¼)in

48(50,52,54)cm / 19(19½,20½,21½)in

(at underarm)
50(55,60,65)cm / 19½(21½,23½,25½)in

Chart

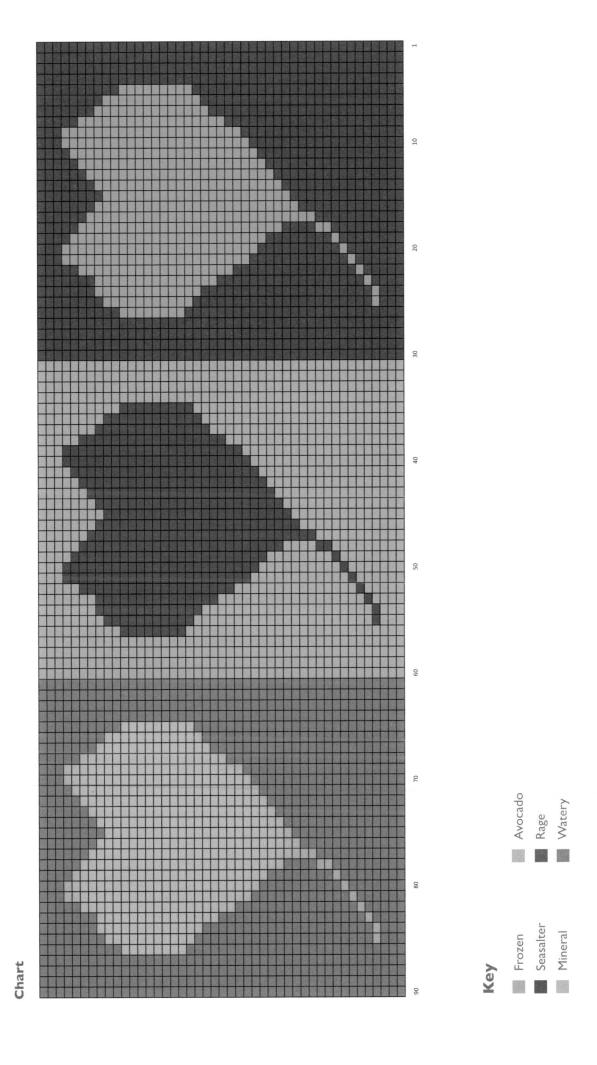

Key

▇ Frozen	▇ Avocado
▇ Seasalter	▇ Rage
▇ Mineral	▇ Watery

hydrangea flower coat

Designed in Rowan Felted Tweed Aran
Carbon (759)
Scree (765)
Cherry (732)

hydrangea
flower coat

SIZE

To fit bust

81-86	91-97	102-107	112-117	cm
32-34	36-38	40-42	44-46	in

Actual bust measurement of garment

92	102	112	122	cm
36¼	40¼	44	48	in

YARN

Rowan Felted Tweed Aran

A Carbon 759

12	14	15	17 x 50gm

B Scree 765

4	4	5	5 x 50gm

C Cherry 732

2	2	2	2 x 50gm

NEEDLES

1 pair 4½mm (no 7) (US 7) needles
1 pair 5mm (no 6) (US 8) needles

EXTRAS

11 buttons

TENSION

16 sts and 23 rows to 10cm / 4in measured over st st, using
5mm (US 8) needles.

BACK

Using 4½mm (US 7) needles and yarn B, cast on
95 (103: 111: 119) sts.
Row 1 (RS): *K1, P1, rep from * to last st, K1.
Row 2: As 2nd row.
These 2 rows form moss st.
Work 4 rows more in moss st.
Break off yarn B, and join in yarn A.

Change to 5mm (US 8) needles.
Cont in moss st until back meas 20cm / 8in, ending with
RS facing for next row.
Cont in st st, dec 1 st at each end of 3rd and 2 foll 8th
rows. 89 (97: 105: 113) sts.
Work 3 rows straight.

Join in yarn B, and work 4 rows straight. Break off yarn B.
Using yarn A, cont in st st, dec 1 st at each end of next and
7 foll 8th rows. 73 [81: 89: 97] sts.
Cont straight until back meas 59 (59.5: 60: 60.5)cm /
23¼ (23½: 23½: 24)in, ending with RS facing for next row.
Break off yarn A, join in yarns B and C.

Beg and ending rows as indicated, using the **intarsia**
technique as described on the information page, and

repeating rows I to 3I throughout, work in patt from chart (**please note:** On first and every foll alt rep of patt, odd-numbered rows are RS rows, but on 2nd and every foll alt rep of patt, odd-numbered rows are **WS** rows), which is worked entirely in st st beg with a K row as folls:
Cont straight until back meas 62.5 (63: 63.5: 64)cm / 24½ (24¾: 25: 25¼)in, ending with RS facing for next row.

Shape armholes
Please note: Armhole shaping is **NOT** shown on the chart.
Cast off 4 (4: 5: 5) sts at beg of next 2 rows.
65 [73: 79: 87] sts.
Dec I st at each end of next I (3: 3: 5) rows, then on foll 2 (3: 4: 5) alt rows. 59 [61: 65: 67] sts.
Cont straight until armhole meas 21 (22.5: 24: 25.5)cm / 8¼ [8¾: 9½: 10]in, ending with RS facing for next row.

Shape shoulders and back neck
Next row (RS): Cast off 6 (6: 7: 7) sts, K until there are 9 (10: 10: 11) sts on right needle and turn, leaving rem sts on a holder.
Work each side of neck separately.
Cast off 4 sts at beg of next row.
Cast off rem 5 (6: 6: 7) sts.
With RS facing, rejoin yarn to rem sts, cast off centre 29 (29: 31: 31) sts, K to end.
Complete to match first side, reversing shapings.

LEFT FRONT
Using 4½mm (US 7) needles and yarn B, cast on 55 (59: 63: 67) sts.
Work 6 rows in moss st as given for back.
Break off yarn B, join in yarn A.

Change to 5mm (US 8) needles.
Cont in moss st until left front meas 20cm / 8in, ending with **WS** facing for next row.
Next row (WS): Moss st 10 sts and slip these sts onto a holder (for button band), MI, moss st to end.
46 [50: 54: 58] sts.
Cont in st st, dec I st at beg (side edge) of 3rd and 2 foll 8th rows. 43 [47: 51: 55] sts.
Work 3 rows straight, ending with RS facing for next row.
Join in yarn B, and work 4 rows straight. Break off yarn B.
Using yarn A, cont in st st, dec I st at side edge of next and 7 foll 8th rows. 35 [39: 43: 47] sts.
Cont straight until left front meas 59 (59.5: 60: 60.5)cm / 23¼ [23½: 23½: 24]in, ending with RS facing for next row.

Break off yarn A, join in yarns B and C.
Beg and ending rows as indicated, using the **intarsia** technique as described on the information page, and repeating rows I to 3I throughout, work in patt from chart (**please note:** On first and every foll alt rep of patt, odd-numbered rows are RS rows, but on 2nd and every foll alt rep of patt, odd-numbered rows are **WS** rows), which is worked entirely in st st beg with a K row as folls:
Cont straight until left front meas 62.5 (63: 63.5: 64)cm / 24½ [24¾: 25: 25¼]in, ending with RS facing for next row.

Shape armhole
Cast off 4 (4: 5: 5) sts at beg of next row. 31 [35: 38: 42] sts.
Work I row.
Dec I st at armhole edge of next I (3: 3: 5) rows, then on foll 2 (3: 4: 5) alt rows. 28 [29: 31: 32] sts.
Cont straight until 26 (26: 28: 28) rows less have been worked than on back to beg of shoulder shaping, ending with RS facing for next row.
Shape front neck
Dec I st at neck edge on next 10 rows, then foll 7 (7: 8: 8) alt rows. 11 [12: 13: 14] sts.
Work 2 rows straight, ending with RS facing for next row.
Shape shoulder
Cast off 6 (6: 7: 7) sts at beg of next row.
Work I row.
Cast off rem 5 (6: 6: 7) sts.
RIGHT FRONT
Using 4½mm (US 7) needles and yarn B, cast on 55 (59: 63: 67) sts.
Work 6 rows in moss st as given for back.
Break off yarn B, join in yarn A.

Change to 5mm (US 8) needles.
Cont in moss st until right front meas 20cm / 8in, ending with **WS** facing for next row.
Next row (WS): Moss st to last 10 sts, MI, and turn leaving rem 10 sts on a holder (for buttonhole band).
46 [50: 54: 58] sts.
Cont in st st, dec I st at end (side edge) of 3rd and 2 foll 8th rows. 43 [47: 51: 55] sts.
Work 3 rows straight, ending with RS facing for next row.
Join in yarn B, and work 4 rows straight. Break off yarn B.
Using yarn A **only**, cont in st st, dec I st at side edge on next and 7 foll 8th rows. 35 [39: 43: 47] sts.
Complete to match left front, reversing shapings.

SLEEVES

Using 4½mm (US 7) needles and yarn B, cast on
45 (47: 49: 51) sts.

Work 6 rows in moss st as given for back.

Break off yarn, join in yarn A.

Change to 5mm (US 8) needles.

Cont in moss st until sleeve meas 15cm / 6in, ending with
RS facing for next row.

Next row (RS): K1, M1, knit to last st, M1, K1.
47 [49: 51: 53] sts.

Last row sets increases.

Working increases as set by last row, beg with a P row
work in st st, inc 1 st at each end of every foll 8th (8th: 6th:
6th) row to 59 (61: 57: 59) sts, then on every foll
– (-: 8th: 8th) row until there are – (-: 65: 67) sts.

Cont straight until sleeve meas 39.5 (39.5: 40.5: 40.5)cm /
15½ (15½: 16: 16)in, ending with RS facing for next row.

Break off yarn A, join in yarns B and C.

Beg and ending rows as indicated, using the **intarsia**
technique as described on the information page, and
repeating rows 1 to 31 throughout, work in patt from
sleeve chart (**please note:** On first and every foll alt rep
of patt, odd-numbered rows are RS rows, but on 2nd and
every foll alt rep of patt, odd-numbered rows are **WS**
rows), which is worked entirely in st st beg with a K row
as folls: Cont straight until sleeve meas 43 (43: 44: 44)cm /
17 (17: 17¼: 17¼)in, ending with RS facing for next row.

Shape top

Please note: Sleeve shaping is **NOT** shown on
the chart.

Cast off 4 (4: 5: 5) sts at beg of next 2 rows.
51 [53: 55: 57] sts.

Dec 1 st at each end of next 3 rows, then on 1 (2: 2: 3) foll alt
rows, then on foll 3 (3: 4: 4) 4th rows. 37 sts.

Work 1 row.

Dec 1 st at each end of next and every foll alt row until
25 sts rem.

Work 1 row.

Cast off 4 sts at beg of next 2 rows.

Cast off rem 17 sts.

MAKING UP

Press as described on the information page.

Join both shoulder seams using mattress stitch.

Button band and collar

Slip 10 sts from left front onto 4½mm (US 7) needles and
rejoin yarn A with RS facing.

Row 1 (RS): (P1, K1) 5 times.

Row 2: (K1, P1) 5 times.

These 2 rows form moss st.

Cont in moss st until button band, when slightly stretched,
fits up left front opening edge, to beg of front slope, sewing
in place as you go **and at same time** working
appropriate colour to match the body, ending with RS facing for
next row.

Collar

Break off all colours except yarn A. Using yarn A only, work
as folls:

Next row (RS): Moss st 1, M1, moss st to end. 11 sts.

This row sets increases for the collar.

Inc 1 st at beg of every foll alt row to 13 sts, then every foll
4th row to 23 sts, taking increase sts into moss st.

Cont straight until collar fits up left front slope and across
to centre back neck, ending with RS facing for next row.

Cast off in moss st.

Mark positions for 11 buttons, first button one to come in
row 6, last button to come 2cm / ¾in below beg of front
slope shaping, and rem 9 buttons evenly spaced between.

Buttonhole band and collar

Slip 10 sts from right front holder onto 4½mm (US 7)
needles and rejoin yarn A with WS facing.

Row 1 (WS): (P1, K1) 5 times.

Row 2: (K1, P1) 5 times.

These 2 rows form moss st.

Work 3 rows in moss st, ending with RS facing for
next row.

Buttonhole row (RS): Patt 5, yon, patt2tog, patt 3.

Complete to match button band, with the addition of a
further 10 buttonholes worked to correspond with
positions marked for buttons, ending with RS facing for
next row.

Collar

Break off all colours except yarn A. Using yarn A only, work
as folls:

Next row (RS): Moss st to last st, M1, moss st 1. 11 sts.

This row sets increases for the collar.

Complete to match collar on button band.

Join cast-off ends of collar and sew in place using mattress
stitch all round left front slope, back neck and right front
slope, reversing sewing for turn back of collar.

Sew in sleeves.

Join side and sleeve seams.

Sew on buttons.

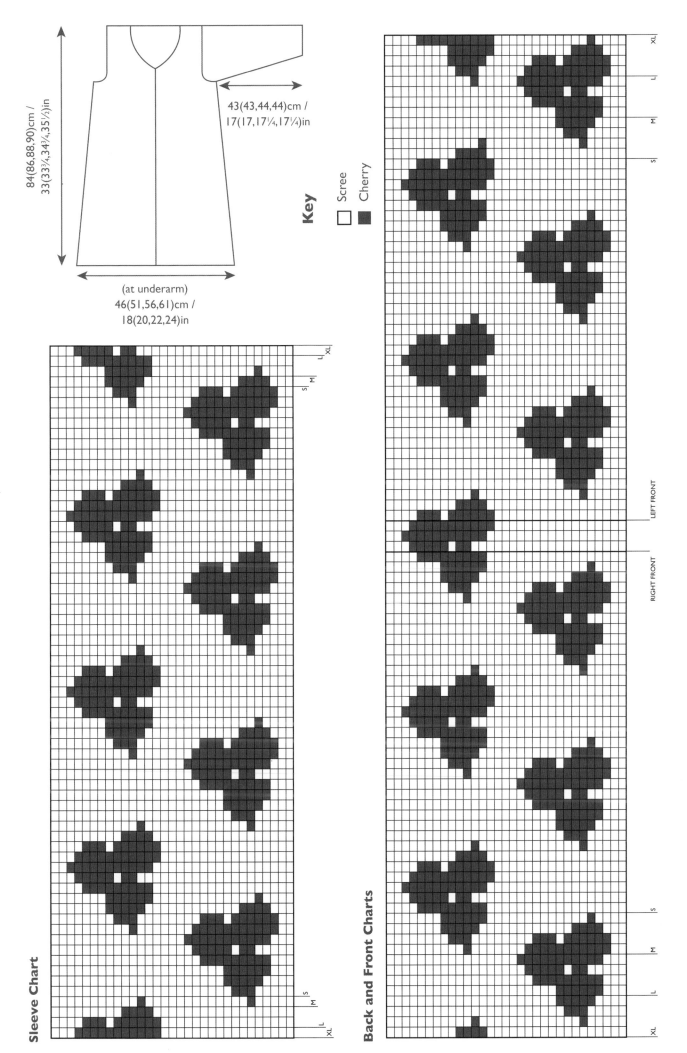

Sleeve Chart

Back and Front Charts

84(86,88,90)cm /
33(33¾,34¾,35½)in

43(43,44,44)cm /
17(17,17¼,17¼)in

(at underarm)
46(51,56,61)cm /
18(20,22,24)in

Key

☐ Scree
■ Cherry

LEFT FRONT

RIGHT FRONT

hydrangea flower hat & scarf

Designed in Rowan Felted Tweed Aran
Carbon (759)
Scree (765)
Cherry (732)

hydrangea flower hat and scarf

SIZE

HAT

To fit an average-size adult woman's head

SCARF

To fit an average-size adult woman's head
Completed scarf (excluding pom poms) measures 22cm / 8¾in by approx.
150cm / 59in.

YARN

Rowan Felted Tweed Aran

Hat

A Carbon 759

2 x 50gm

B Scree 765

1 x 50gm

C Cherry 732

1 x 50gm

Scarf

A Carbon 759

2 x 50gm

B Scree 765

2 x 50gm

C Cherry 732

2 x 50gm

NEEDLES

1 pair 4½mm (no 7) (US 7) needles for hat only.
1 pair 5mm (no 6) (US 8) needles.

TENSION

16 sts and 23 rows to 10cm / 4in measured over st st, using
5mm (US 8) needles.

HAT

Using 4½mm (US 7) needles and yarn A, cast on 86 sts.

Row 1 (RS): *P2, K2, rep from * to last 2 sts, P2.
Row 2: K2, *P2, K2, rep from * to end.
These 2 rows form rib.
Cont in rib until hat meas 15cm / 6in, ending with **WS**
facing for next row.
Next row (WS): Purl to end, dec 1 st in centre of row.
85 sts.
Break off yarn A, join in yarn B.

Change to 5mm (US 6) needles.

Beg and ending rows as indicated, using the **intarsia** technique as described on the information page, work rows 1 to 20 from hat chart **once**, repeating the 17-st patt rep 5 times across each row, which is worked entirely in st st beg with a K row.

Break off yarns B and C. Join in yarn A.

Next row: K to end.

Cont as folls:

Row 1 (WS): *K1, P1, rep from * to last st, K1.

Row 2: As row 1.

These 2 rows form moss st.

Working in moss st cont as folls:

Work 1 row, ending with RS facing for next row.

Shape crown

Row 1 (RS): Patt 1, (patt3tog, patt 9) 7 times. 71 sts.

Work 5 rows straight.

Row 7: Patt 1, (patt3tog, patt 7) 7 times. 57 sts.

Work 3 rows straight.

Row 11: Patt 1, (patt3tog, patt 5) 7 times. 43 sts.

Work 3 rows straight.

Row 15: Patt 1, (patt3tog, patt 3) 7 times. 29 sts.

Work 3 rows straight.

Row 19: Patt 1, (patt3tog, patt 1) 7 times. 15 sts.

Work 1 row straight.

Row 21st: Patt 1, (patt2tog) 7 times. 8 sts.

Break yarn and thread through rem 8 sts.

Pull up tight and fasten off securely.

MAKING UP

Using mattress stitch, join back seam, reversing sewing for turnback.

Using yarn C, make a 9cm / 3½in diameter pom pom, and attach to centre of crown.

SCARF

First side

Using 5mm (US 6) needles and yarn B, cast on 33 sts.

Row 1 (RS): K1, *P1, K1, rep from * to end.

Row 2: As row 2.

These 2 rows form moss st.

Work 4 rows more in moss st.

Break off yarn B, and join in yarn A.

Cont in moss st until scarf meas 14cm / 5½in, ending with RS facing for next row.

Break off yarn A, join in yarns B and C.

Beg and ending rows as indicated, using the **intarsia** technique as described on the information page, work rows 1 to 36 from scarf chart **once**, which is worked entirely in st st beg with a K row.

Break off yarns B and C. Join in yarn A.

Cont in st st until scarf meas 43.5cm / 17¼in, ending with RS facing for next row.

Join in yarn B, and work 4 rows in st st, ending with RS facing for next row.

Break off yarn B.

Using yarn A, cont in st st until scarf meas 75cm / 29½in, ending with RS facing for next row. Leave sts on a holder.

Second side

Work to match first side.

Join both sets of 33 sts to form back seam either by grafting sts tog or by casting off both sets of sts tog.

Using yarn C, make 10 pom poms approx 4cm / 1½in diameter. Attach evenly to cast-on and cast-off edges.

Scarf Chart

Key

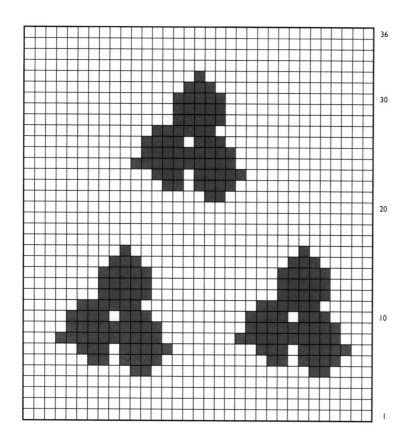

☐ Scree

■ Cherry

36

30

20

10

1

Hat Chart

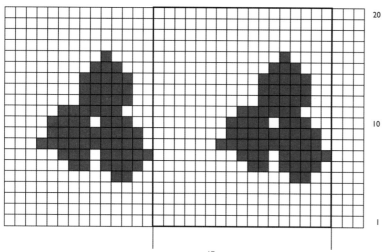

20

10

1

17 st patt repeat

oak leaf
yoke top

Designed in Rowan Felted Tweed
Pine (158)
Avocado (161)
Rage (150)

oak leaf yoke top

SIZE

To fit bust

81-86	91-97	102-107	112-117	cm
32-34	36-38	40-42	44-46	in

Actual bust measurement of garment

90	101	110	121	cm
35½	39¾	43¼	47¾	in

YARN

Rowan Felted Tweed

A Pine 158

3	3	4	4 x 50gm

B Avocado 161

1	1	1	1 x 50gm

C Rage 150

1	1	1	1 x 50gm

NEEDLES

1 pair 3¼mm (no 10) (US 3) needles.

1 pair 4mm (no 8) (US 6) needles

1 3¼mm (no 10) (US 3) circular needle 40cm long.

1 4mm (no 8) (US 6) circular needle, one 60cm long and one 40cm long.

TENSION

22 sts and 30 rows to 10 cm measured over st st, using 4mm (US 6) needles.

EXTRAS

Stitch holder.

BACK and FRONT (both alike)

Using 3¼mm (US 2) needles and yarn B, cast on 85 (97: 107: 119) sts.

Row 1 (RS): K1, *P1, K1, rep from * to end.

Row 2: *P1, K1, rep from * to last st, P1.

These 2 rows form rib.

Work 1 row more.

Break off yarn B, join in yarn A.

Next row (WS): Purl.

Using yarn A, cont in rib until work meas 9cm / 3½in, ending with RS facing for next row.

Change to 4mm (US 6) needles.

Row 1 (RS): Knit.

Row 2: K1, purl to last st, K1.

Last 2 rows form st st with edge sts.

Cont as set as folls:

Work 6 rows, ending with RS facing for next row.

Next row (RS): K1, M1, knit to last st, M1, K1.

87 [99: 109: 121] sts.

Last row sets increases.

Working increases as set by last row, inc 1 st at each end of every foll 8th row to 99 (109: 117: 127) sts, then on every foll – (10th: 10th: 10th) row until – (111: 121: 133) sts.

Work 1 row straight, ending with RS facing for next row. Place markers at both ends of last row to denote base of armhole openings.

Cont straight until work meas 9 (10: 11: 12)cm / 3½ (4: 4¼: 4¾)in from markers, ending with RS facing for next row.

Shape neck

Next row (RS): K23 (26: 31: 35) and turn, leaving rem sts on a holder.

Work each side of neck separately.

Dec 1 st at neck edge on next 6 rows. 17 [20: 25: 29] sts.

Work 1 row straight, ending with RS facing for next row.

Shape shoulder

Dec 1 st at neck edge on next and 2 (3: 4: 5) foll alt rows **and at same time** cast off 3 (3: 3: 3) sts at beg of next and foll 1 (3: 3: 4) alt row, then 4 (-: 4: 4) sts on foll 1 (-: 1: 1) rows. 4 [4: 4: 4] sts.

Work 1 row straight.

Cast off rem sts.

Back

With RS facing, slip first 27 (30, 30, 32) sts onto a stitch holder place a marker on the last stitch (this denotes centre back), then slip next 26(29, 29, 31) sts onto a second stitch holder, rejoin yarn A to rem sts, K to end.

Complete to match first side, reversing shapings.

Front

With RS facing, slip centre 53 [59: 59: 63] sts onto a holder placing a marker on centre st

(this denotes centre back or front neck), rejoin yarn A, to rem sts, K to end.

Complete to match first side, reversing shapings.

MAKING UP

Press as described on the information page.

Join both shoulder seams using back stitch, or mattress stitch if preferred.

Yoke and neckband

With RS facing, using longer 4mm (US 6) circular needle and yarn A, beg at first st after centre st of centre back neck st, knit 26 (29: 29: 31) sts from second back neck

stitch holder, pick up and knit 18 (20: 20: 22) sts up left side of back neck, pick up and knit 18 [20: 20: 22] sts down left side of front neck, knit 53 (59: 59: 63) sts from front neck stitch holder, pick up and knit 19 (20: 20: 23) sts up right side of front neck, pick up and knit 19 (20: 20: 23) sts down right side of back neck, then knit 27 (30: 30: 32) sts from first back neck stitch holder, ending at centre st. 180 [198: 198: 216] sts.

Using the **Fair Isle/intarsia** technique as described on the information page, repeating the 18-st patt rep 10 [11: 11: 12] times around each round, work rows 1 to 20 in patt from chart **once**, which is worked entirely in st st (K every round).

Break off yarns B and C.

Using A **only**, work as folls, changing to shorter 4mm (US 6) circular needle when required:

Round 1: (K3, K2tog, K4) 20 (22: 22: 24) times. 160 [176: 176: 192] sts.

Round 2: Knit.

Round 3: (K6, K2tog) 20 (22: 22: 24) times. 140 [154: 154: 168] sts.

Round 4: Knit.

Round 5: (K2, K2tog, K3) 20 (22: 22: 24) times. 120 [132: 132: 144] sts.

Change to 3¼mm (US 3) circular needle.

Round 1: *K1, P1, rep from * to end.

Rep round 1, 7 times more.

Break off yarn A, join in yarn B.

Next round: Knit.

Rep this round once.

Cast off in rib.

Armhole borders (both alike)

With RS facing, using 3¼mm (US 3) needles and yarn A, pick up and knit 51(55: 59: 63) sts evenly along armhole opening edge between markers.

Beg with row 2, work in rib as given for back and front for 7 rows.

Break off yarn A, join in yarn B.

Next row: Knit.

Work 1 row in rib.

Cast off in rib.

Join side and armhole border seams, using mattress stitch.

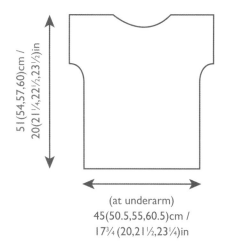

51(54,57,60)cm /
20(21¼,22½,23½)in

(at underarm)
45(50.5,55,60.5)cm /
17¾ (20,21½,23¼)in

Chart

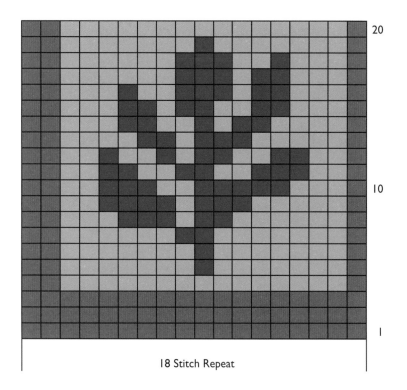

20

10

1

18 Stitch Repeat

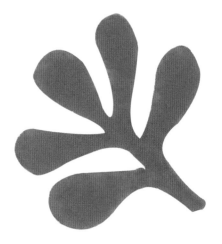

Key

- ■ Pine
- ■ Avocado
- ■ Rage

pom pom shawl

Designed in Rowan Valley Tweed
Littondale (102)
Bedale (106)
Wolds Poppy (107)
Gordale (105)

pom pom
shawl

SIZE

One size

212cm / 83½in x 50cm / 19¾in (excluding pom poms)

YARN

Rowan Valley Tweed

A Littondale 102
4 x 50gm

B Bedale 106
2 x 50gm

C Wolds Poppy 107
2 x 50gm

D Gordale 105
1 x 50gm

NEEDLES

1 pair 3¼mm (no 10) (US 3) needles.

TENSION

24 sts and 36 rows to 10cm / 4in measured over st st, using 3¼mm (US 3) needles.

EXTRAS

Pom pom maker.

Read through the entire pattern before beginning as chart is placed.

Using yarn A, cast on 8 sts.
Row 1 (RS): Sl 1, K to last 5 sts, M1, (K1, P1) twice, K1.
Row 2: (K1, P1) twice, K1, P to end.
Row 3: Sl 1, K to last 5 sts, (K1, P1) twice, K1.
Row 4: As row 2.
Row 5: As row 1.
Row 6: As row 2.
Rep last 6 rows, 55 times more. 120 sts.

Next row (RS): Sl 1, K to last 5 sts, (K1, P1) twice, K1.
Next row: (K1, P1) twice, K1, P to end.
Rep last 2 rows 52 times more.

Next row (RS): Sl 1, K to last 7 sts, K2tog, (K1, P1) twice, K1.
Next row: (K1, P1) twice, K1, P to end.
Next row: Sl 1, K to last 5sts, (K1, P1) twice, K1.
Next row: (K1, P1) twice, K1, P to end.
Next row: Sl 1, K to last 7sts, K2tog, (K1, P1) twice, K1.
Next row: (K1, P1) twice, K1, P to end.
Rep last 6 rows to 8sts.
And **at the same time**, using the **intarsia** technique as described on the information page, place chart as folls:

Row 51: Sl 1, work 4 sts, work row 1 of chart. Work rem rows of chart as placed on next 12 rows.
Row 121: Sl 1, work 7 sts, place chart.
Row 175: Sl 1, work 7 sts, place chart.
Row 193: Sl 1, work 43 sts, place chart
Row 247: Sl 1, work 30 sts, place chart.
Row 277: Sl 1, work 73 sts, place chart.
Row 307: Sl 1, work 6 sts, place chart.
Row 365: Sl 1, work 51 sts, place chart.
Row 385: Sl 1, work 95 sts, place chart.
Row 415: Sl 1, work 25 sts, place chart.
Row 451: Sl 1, work 65 sts, place chart.
Row 499: Sl 1, work 36 sts, place chart.
Row 529: Sl 1, work 70 sts, place chart.
Row 565: Sl 1, work 9 sts, place chart.
Row 617: Sl 1, work 33 sts, place chart.
Row 661: Sl 1, work 12 sts, place chart.
Row 709: Sl 1, work 9 sts, place chart.
Cast off.

MAKING UP

Press as described on the information page.

Make 61 pom poms approx 4cm / 1.5in in diameter, 30 in yarn B and 31 in yarn C, leaving a length of yarn approx 12cm/4¾in long on each pom pom.

Use a tapestry needle to attach the pom pom to the moss stitch edge of the shawl.

Bring the needle back through the centre of the pom pom, pulling the yarn so the pom pom sits as close to the shawl edge as possible.

Fasten off and rep for rem pom poms.

Chart

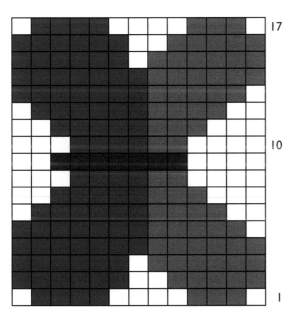

Key

■ Bedale
■ Wolds Poppy
■ Gordale
☐ Littondale

spring blossom cardigan

Designed in Rowan Alpaca Soft DK
Rainy Day (210)
Toffee (203)
Deep Rose (206)
Clover (215)

spring blossom cardigan

SIZE

To fit bust

81-86	91-97	102-107	112-117	cm
32-34	36-38	40-42	44-46	in

Actual bust measurement of garment

126	135	146	155	cm
49½	53¼	57½	61	in

YARN

Alpaca soft dk

A Rainy Day 210

11	12	12	13	x 50gm

B Toffee 203

2	2	2	2	x 50gm

C Deep Rose 206

1	1	1	1	x 50gm

D Clover 215

1	1	1	1	x 50gm

NEEDLES

1 pair 3¾mm (no 9) (US 5) needles

1 pair 4mm (no 8) (US 6) needles

3¾mm (no 9) (US 5) circular needle at least 80cm/
31½in long.

TENSION

22 sts and 30 rows to 10 cm/4in measured over st st, using
4mm (US 6) needles.

BACK

Using 3¾mm (US 5) needles and yarn B, cast on
138 (150: 162: 170) sts.

Row 1 (RS): K2, *P2, K2, rep from * to end.

Row 2: *P2, K2, rep from * to last 2 sts, P2.

These 2 rows form rib.

Cont in rib until back meas 9cm/3¼in, inc (dec: dec: inc)
1 st at end of last row, and ending with **WS** facing for next
row. 139 [149: 161: 171] sts.

Next row (WS): K1, purl to last st, K1.

Break off yarn B, and join in yarn A.

Change to 4mm (US 6) needles.

Row 1 (RS): Knit.

Row 2: K1, purl to last st, K1.

Last 2 rows form st st with edge sts.

Cont straight as set until back meas 73.5 (75.5: 77.5: 79.5)cm
/ 29(29¾: 30½: 31¼)in, ending with RS facing for next row.

Shape shoulders and back neck

Next row (RS): Cast off 24 (27: 29: 32) sts, K until there
are 28(30: 33: 35) sts on right needle and turn, leaving rem
sts on a holder.

Work each side of neck separately.

Cast off 4 sts at beg of next row.

Cast off rem 24 (26: 29: 31) sts.

With RS facing, rejoin yarn A, to rem sts, cast off centre 35 (35: 37: 37) sts, K to end.

Complete to match first side, reversing shapings.

LEFT FRONT

Using 3¾mm (US 5) needles and yarn B, cast on 67 (71: 79: 83) sts.

Row 1 (RS): K2, *P2, K2, rep from * to last st, P1.

Row 2: K1, *P2, K2, rep from * to last 2 sts, P2.

These 2 rows form rib.

Cont in rib until left front meas 9cm/3¼in, – (inc: dec: -) – (1: 1: -) st at end of last row, and ending with **WS** facing for next row. 67 [72: 78: 83] sts.

Next row (WS): Purl to last st, K1.

Break off yarn B, and join in yarn A.

Change to 4mm (US 6) needles.

Row 1 (RS): Knit.

Row 2: Purl to last st, K1.

Last 2 rows form st st with edge st.

Cont straight as set until 92 (94: 98: 100) rows less have been worked than on back to beg of shoulder shaping, ending with RS facing for next row.

Place motif chart

Using the **intarsia** technique as described on the information page, now place patt from motif chart for left front, which is worked entirely in st st beg with a K row as folls:

Next Row (RS): K1 (3: 6: 10), work next 59 sts as row 1 of motif chart, K7 (10: 13: 14).

Next Row. P7 (10: 13: 14), work next 59 sts as row 2 of motif chart, P1 (3: 6: 10).

These 2 rows set the sts – chart for left front with st st in yarn A at each side.

Keeping sts correct throughout as now set, work 24 rows, ending with RS facing for next row.

Shape front slope

(Note: Front sloping is **NOT** shown on the chart).

Keeping patt correct, dec 1 st at end of next and 6 foll 4th rows. 60 [65: 71: 76] sts.

Work 3 rows, ending after chart row 54. (All 54 rows of motif chart are now completed).

Now working all sts in st st using yarn A **only**, cont as folls:

Dec 1 st at end on next and 4 (5: 6: 7) foll 4th rows, then on foll 7 (6: 6: 5) alt rows. 48 [53: 58: 63] sts.

Work 7 rows straight, ending with RS facing for next row.

Shape shoulder

Cast off 24 (27: 29: 32) sts at beg of next row.

Work 1 row.

Cast off rem 24 (26: 29: 31) sts.

RIGHT FRONT

Using 3¾mm (US 5) needles and yarn B, cast on 67 (71: 79: 83) sts.

Row 1 (RS): P1, K2, *P2, K2, rep from * to end.

Row 2: *P2, K2, rep from * to last 3 sts, P2, K1.

These 2 rows form rib.

Cont in rib until right front meas 9cm/3¼in, - (inc: dec: -) – (1: 1: -) st at beg of last row, and ending with **WS** facing for next row. 67 [72: 78: 83] sts.

Next row (WS): K1, purl to end.

Break off yarn B, and join in yarn A.

Change to 4mm (US 6) needles.

Row 1 (RS): Knit.

Row 2: K1, purl to end.

Last 2 rows form st st with edge st.

Complete to match left front, reversing all shapings and ignoring all reference to chart (by working this front in yarn A **only)**.

SLEEVES

Using 3¾mm (US 5) needles and yarn B, cast on 46 (46: 50: 50) sts.

Work 36 rows in rib as given for back as folls:

Work 8 rows, ending with RS facing for next row.

Row 9 (RS): Rib 1, M1, rib to last st, M1, rib 1.

48 [48: 52: 52] sts.

Last row sets increases.

Working increases as set by last row, inc 1 st at each end on 3 (4: 4: 4) foll 8th (6th: 6th: 6th) rows. 54 [56: 60: 60] sts.

Work 2 rows, ending with WS facing for next row.

Next row (WS): K1, purl to last st, K1.

Break off yarn B, join in yarn A.

Change to 4mm (US 6) needles.

Cont in st st with edges as given on Back as folls:

Work 4 [2:2:2] rows, ending with RS facing for next row.

Next row (RS): K1, M1, knit to last st, M1, K1.

56 [58: 62: 62] sts.

Last row sets increases.

Working increases as set by last row, inc 1 st at each end

of on every foll 8th (6th: 6th: 6th) row to 68 (60: 68: 84) sts, then on every foll 10th (8th: 8th: 8th) row until there are 74 (78: 84: 88) sts.

Cont straight until sleeve meas 43 [43: 44: 44]cm/ 17(17:17¼:17¼)in, ending with RS facing for next row.

Shape top

Cast off 8 sts at beg of next 8 (6: 2: -) rows.

Cast off – (9: 9: 9) sts at beg of next -(2: 6: 8) rows.

Cast off rem 10 (12: 14: 16) sts.

MAKING UP

Press as described on the information page.

Join shoulder seams using mattress stitch.

Right Front Collar

Using 3¾mm (US 5) needles and yarn A, cast on 1 st.

Work as folls:

Next row (RS): K1.

Next row: Inc in st. 2 sts.

Next row: K1, M1, K1. 3 sts.

Next row: P1, M1, P2. 4 sts.

Next row: K3, M1, K1. 5 sts.

Working increases as set by last row, and working in st st throughout inc 1 st at the same edge on foll 2 rows, then on foll 16 alt rows. 23 sts.

Work 1 row straight, ending with RS facing for next row.

Place motif chart

Using the **intarsia** technique as described on the information page, now place patt from motif chart for right front collar front, which is worked entirely in st st beg with a K row as folls:

Next Row (RS): K2, K1, work next 16 sts as row 1 of motif chart, knit to last st, M1, K1. 24 sts.

Next Row. Purl to last 18 sts, work next 16 sts as row 2 of motif chart, P2.

These 2 rows set the sts – chart for right front collar with st st in yarn A at each side.

Keeping sts correct throughout as now set, work 12 rows inc 1 st on next and foll 2 alt rows, then on foll 4th row, ending with RS facing for next row. 28 sts.

Inc 1 st at end of next and 2 foll 4th rows. 31 sts.

Cont straight until collar is of sufficient length to go up front slope to shoulder, when slightly stretched, ending with RS facing for next row.

Cast off 16 sts at beg of next row. 15 sts.

Working on these 15 sts, cont until collar is of sufficient length to go halfway across back neck when slightly

stretched, ending with RS facing for next row.

Cast off.

Right front collar edging

With RS facing, using 3¾mm (US 5) needles and yarn B, beg at 16 cast-off sts, pick up and knit 50 (50: 54: 54) sts down edge of collar.

Next Row (WS): Purl.

Beg with row 1 of rib as given for back, work 11 rows.

Cast off in rib.

Left front collar

Using 3¾mm (US 5) needles and yarn A, cast on 1 st.

Work as folls:

Next row (RS): K1.

Next row: Inc in st. 2 sts.

Next row: K1, M1, K1. 3 sts.

Next row. P2, M1, P1. 4 sts.

Next row: K1, M1, K3. 5 sts.

Working increases as set by last row, inc 1 st at same edge on foll 2 rows, then on foll 16 alt rows. 23 sts.

Complete to match right front collar, reversing all shapings and ignoring all reference to chart (by working this collar in yarn A **only)**.

Left front collar edging

With RS facing, using 3¾mm (US 5) needles and yarn B, pick up and knit 50 (50: 54: 54) sts up side edge of collar to 16 cast-off sts.

Next Row (WS): Purl.

Beg with row 1 of rib as given for back, work 11 rows.

Cast off in rib.

Right front border

With RS facing, using 3¾mm (US 5) circular needle and yarn B, beg at front cast-on edge pick up and knit 138 (142: 146: 150) sts up right front opening, ending at beg of front slope.

Next row (WS): Purl.

Beg with row 1 of rib as given for back, work 11 rows.

Cast off in rib.

Left front border

With RS facing, using 3¾mm (US 5) circular needle and yarn B, beg at front slope, pick up and knit 138 (142: 146: 150) sts down left front opening, ending at cast-on edge.

Next row (WS): Purl.

Beg with row 1 of rib as given for back, work 11 rows.

Cast off in rib.

Patch pockets (Make 2)

Using 3¾mm (US 5) needles and yarn A, cast on 20 sts.

Beg with a K row, cont in st st as folls:

Work 2 rows, ending with RS facing for next row.

Next row (RS): K1, M1, knit to last st, M1, K1. 22 sts.

Working increases as set by last row, inc 1 st at each end on 3 foll alt rows. 28 sts.

Work 3 rows straight.

Place motif chart

Using the **intarsia** technique as described on the information page, now place patt from motif chart for pocket, which is worked entirely in st st beg with a K row as folls:

Next Row (RS): K6, work next 16 sts as row 1 of motif chart, K6.

Next Row. P6, work next 16 sts as row 2 of motif chart, P6.

These 2 rows set the sts – chart for pocket with st st in yarn A at each side.

Keeping sts correct throughout as now set, work 12 rows, ending with RS facing for next row.

Break off yarns B, C and D.

Using yarn A **only w**ork 8 rows straight.

Cast off.

Using mattress stitch, join cast-off ends of collar and placing seam to centre back neck sew in place all round left front slope, back neck and right front slope, reversing sewing for collar.

Join front borders and collar edging seams.

Mark points along side seam edges 18 (19: 20: 21) cm either side of shoulder seams (to denote base of armhole openings), sew in sleeves.

Using mattress stitch, join side and sleeve seams.

Sew on pockets as illustrated.

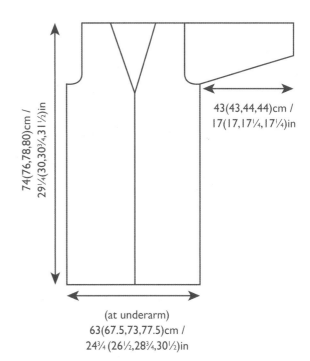

43(43,44,44)cm /
17(17,17¼,17¼)in

74(76,78,80)cm /
29¼(30,30¾,31½)in

(at underarm)
63(67.5,73,77.5)cm /
24¾(26½,28¾,30½)in

Main Chart

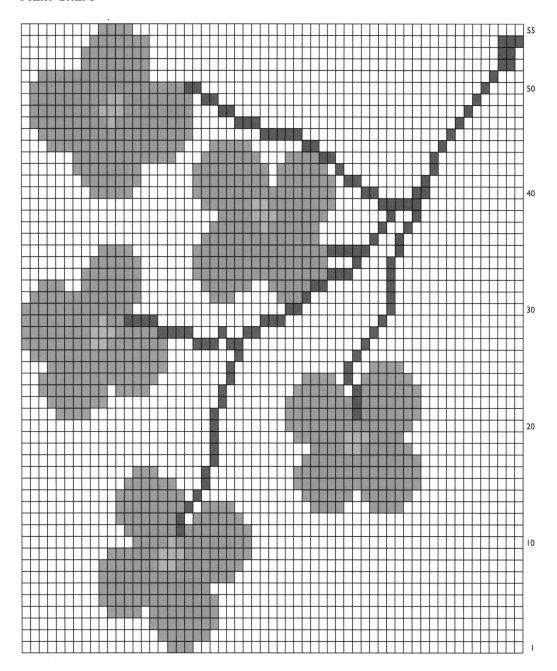

Pockets and Right Front Collar Chart

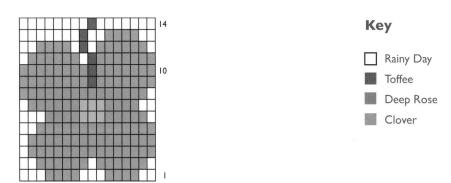

Key

☐ Rainy Day

■ Toffee

▦ Deep Rose

▥ Clover

boyfriend sweater
in alpaca soft dk
by Dee Hardwicke

ribs
Long sleeves
Left turn
up

When Richard & I lived in Bath
before we were married we loved
going for long rambling walks
in the beautiful city parks. There's
nothing nicer to keep me warm on
winter days & the cool summers than
being wrapped up in one of Richard's hand knit sweaters.
My boyfriend sweater is inspired by those romantic city park walks
& the flowers in bloom that decorated our path.

Dee Hardwicke

---

circle flowers sweater
in valley tweed
by Dee Hardwicke

When I was very young we lived in
South Orange, New Jersey. On Sunday
afternoons I would sit on the front
lawn with my big pad of paper, pencils
and paint and I drew the things
around me — flowers, trees, leaves, houses
and birds. I loved to draw the rows
of flowers that lined my neighbor's front
garden. My Circle Flowers sweater
celebrates those happy childhood drawings.

from a little oak leaf I
found when playing in the
park with my son when
he was very small. I love
this little oak leaf and it
has inspired many designs.

Dee Hardwicke

information

CHART NOTE

The patterns in this book are worked from charts. Each square on a chart represents a stitch and each line of squares a row of knitting. Each colour used is given a different letter and these are shown in the materials section, or in the key alongside the chart of each pattern. When working from the charts, read odd rows (K) from right to left and even rows (P) from left to right, unless otherwise stated.

KNITTING WITH COLOUR

There are two main methods of working colour into a knitted fabric. Intarsia and Fair Isle techniques. The first method produces a single thickness of fabric and is usually used where a colour is only required in a particular area of a row and does not form a repeating pattern across the row, as in the Fair Isle technique.

Fair Isle Knitting; When two or three colours are worked repeatedly across a row, strand the yarn not in use loosely behind the stitches being worked. If you are working with more than two colours, treat the "floating" yarns as if they were one yarn and always spread the stitches to their width to keep them elastic. It is advisable not to carry the stranded or "floating" yarns over more than three stitches at a time, but to weave them under and over the colour you are working. The "floating" yarns are therefore caught at the back of the work.

Intarsia; The intarsia technique is used to create pictures with yarn. As an artist and knitter, I love this technique, as it works beautifully for translating my paintings and designs into richly coloured knitted motifs. When working in intarsia you've the freedom to use as few as two colours, or as many colours as your design needs.

When you come to change colour you just need to make sure that you secure the old yarn, the yarn that you're knitting with, with the new yarn, the yarn you're about to pick up. Securing the old yarn with the new yarn will avoid any unwanted holes in your intarsia design.

When you come to a new colour on your chart, the yarn you're knitting with becomes your old yarn and the one you're picking up is your new yarn. Put the old yarn over the new yarn that you're about to pick up and pick up the new yarn from underneath the old yarn - you've now captured the old yarn with the new yarn eliminating the possibility of a hole.

abbreviations

K – knit

P – purl

St(s) – stitch(es)

cm – centimetres

in – inches

RS – right side

WS – wrong side

Meas – measures

Inc – increase

Dec – decrease

St st – stocking stitch (1 row K, 1 row P)

G st – garter stitch (K every row)

Beg – begin(ning)

Foll – following

Folls – follows

Rem – remain(ing)

Rep – repeat

Alt – alternate

Cont – continue

Patt – pattern

Tog – together

Sl 1 – slip one stitch

Psso – pass slipped stitch over

Yon – yarn over needle or yarn round needle
(makes 1 stitch)

M1 – make 1 stitch by picking up horizontal loop
before next stitch and knitting into back of it

0 – no stitches, times or rows

- no stitches, times or rows for that size

sizing guide

STANDARD SIZING GUIDE FOR WOMEN

The sizing within this chart is based on the larger size within the range, ie. M will be based on size 14.

UK SIZE	S	M	L	XL	
DUAL SIZE	8/10	12/14	16/18	20/22	
To fit bust	32 – 34	36 – 38	40 – 42	44 – 46	inches
	81 – 86	91 - 97	102 – 107	112 – 117	cm
To fit waist	24 – 26	28 – 30	32 – 34	36 – 38	inches
	61 – 66	71 – 76	81 – 86	91 – 97	cm
To fit hips	34 – 36	38 – 40	42 – 44	46 – 48	inches
	86 – 91	97 – 102	107 – 112	117 – 122	cm

BUST —
WAIST —
HIPS —

SIZING & SIZE DIAGRAM NOTE

The instructions are given for the smallest size. Where they vary, work the figures in brackets for the larger sizes. One set of figures refers to all sizes. Included with most patterns in this publication is a 'size diagram' - see image on the right, of the finished garment and its dimensions. The measurement shown at the bottom of each 'size diagram' shows the garment width 2.5cm below the armhole shaping. To help you choose the size of garment to knit please refer to the sizing guide. Generally in the majority of designs the welt width (at the cast on edge of the garment) is the same width as the chest. However, some designs are 'A-Line' in shape or flared edge and in these cases welt width will be wider than the chest width.

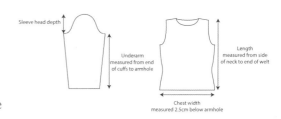

Sleeve head depth

Underarm measured from end of cuffs to armhole

Length measured from side of neck to end of welt

Chest width measured 2.5cm below armhole

MEASURING GUIDE

For maximum comfort and to ensure the correct fit when choosing a size to knit, please follow the tips below when checking your size. Measure yourself close to your body, over your underwear and don't pull the tape measure too tight!

BUST/CHEST – measure around the fullest part of the bust/chest and across the shoulder blades.

WAIST – measure around the natural waistline, just above the hip bone.

HIPS – measure around the fullest part of the bottom.

If you don't wish to measure yourself, note the size of a favourite jumper that you like the fit of.
Measure your favourite jumper and then compare these measurements with the size diagram given at the end of the individual instructions.
Finally, once you have decided which size is best for you, please ensure that you achieve the tension required for the design you wish to knit. Remember if your tension is too loose, your garment will be bigger than the pattern size and you may use more yarn. If your tension is too tight, your garment could be smaller than the pattern size and you will have yarn left over.

Furthermore if your tension is incorrect, the handle of your fabric will be too stiff or floppy and will not fit properly. It really does make sense to check your tension before starting every project.

pom poms

about the author

Dee Hardwicke is an artist, designer and knitter with
a rich and diverse portfolio inspired by her love
of the British landscape. Whether Dee is creating
knitwear, stationery, or ceramics for the National Trust,
her designs begin life in her sketchbooks, where she
records all of the beautiful details that catch her eye
throughout the seasons.

A passionate believer in creating accessible pieces
which celebrate nature and add joy and colour to
everyday life, Dee loves translating her sketches into
designs for stunning knits that will be treasured for
years to come. This passion gave rise to Dee's previous
book, 'A Story in Yarn: How to Design and Knit an
Intarsia Heirloom Quilt (Quail)', and now 'Colourwork
Knits' features Dee's debut knitwear collection.

Based in the Welsh countryside, Dee holds regular
intarsia design workshops throughout the UK in
venues such as Liberty, London. Please visit
www.deehardwicke.co.uk for details of Dee's
latest workshops, products and events.

acknowledgements

I love the process of working with different materials to create pieces that are both beautiful and useful. I find the rhythmic quality of knitting, and the joy of working with beautiful yarns, a wonderful way of slowing down and reconnecting with the pleasure of making something by hand. I've had so much fun designing this debut knitwear collection, and I hope you enjoy knitting your favourite patterns, either for yourself or as really special gifts for friends and family.

I'd like to say a huge thank you to all of the very talented knitters who brought my designs to life for this book. Thank you for your beautiful knitting, attention to detail and invaluable maths skills!

Jane Bradbury
Trish Bunyan
Rae Chapman
Amanda Golland
Jane Harvey
Kate Hudson
Mary Leeson
Carolyn Mace
Harriet Wheelock

A very big thank you to flower farmer Georgie Newbery and artist Fabrizio Bocca for welcoming us to your beautiful flower farm in Somerset. Common Farm Flowers (www.commonfarmflowers.com) are specialist growers and suppliers of English country flowers, and this gorgeous setting was the perfect location for the 'Colourwork Knits' shoot. Georgie, Fabrizio and the wonderful team made the shoot really special!

Thank you Jesse Wild (jessewild.co.uk) for your beautiful photography and sensitivity.

Thank you Elizabeth of Mar for your continuing support, encouragement and for your keen eye and patience when reading and rereading drafts!

And thank you to my wonderful publisher and the entire Quail team for allowing me so much creative freedom, for your expertise and for making the process of creating a book so enjoyable!